THE GREATNESS OF BLACK WOMEN

ALL THE REASONS WHY WE *LOVE SISTERS*

PERSONAL OPINIONS FROM THE BLACK MEN WHO LOVE THEM

BY KEVIN WAINE, M.A.

ILLUSTRATIONS BY SUMAKU GOLSTON

HATS OFF™

AUSTIN BRANCH
5615 W. RACE AVENUE
CHICAGO, ILLINOIS 60644

The Greatness of Black Women:
All the Reasons Why We Love Sisters.
Copyright © 2003 by Kevin Waine

All rights reserved. No part of this book may
be reproduced or transmitted in any form or
by any means without the written consent
of the publisher.

Published by Hats Off Books™
610 East Delano Street, Suite 104
Tucson, Arizona 85705

ISBN: 1-58736-197-3
LCCN: 2003091849

Illustrations by Sumaku Golston.

Acknowledgments

I could not have written this book had it not been for my family, friends, and the many lovely ladies that I am proud to call my friends. When I needed an understanding, loving ear, they were there; when I needed spiritual healing, they were there; and when I felt alone, my wonderful friends kept me company. So I say to all of you, and you certainly know who you are, thank you, thank you, thank you for your love and support.

There are so many other people who deserve my gratitude and love. After the death of my wife, I found myself being encouraged by family and friends to start dating again. However, I quickly realized that I in fact had absolutely NO experience dating due to the length of time Melessa and I had been married. I also quickly began to learn some very hard lessons. I learned that my platonic lady friends were some of my best teachers. Through endless hours of conversation, they schooled me on the dos and don'ts of dating. My friend Sharon would talk to me for hours and hours in order to help me understand why someone would treat me so badly when all I wanted to do was treat them with respect, love, and care.

Another close friend, Lesley, would always call me if she hadn't heard from me for a while and say,

"Hey boo, what the hell is up with you, are you OK?" I guess what I'm trying to say is that through these ladies and others, like Karen, Debra, Trina and my cousins Tonya, Cookie and Rhonda, I was able to heal my spirit. However, something happened during that healing process. I learned how hard it is for a black woman-sister to keep her hope alive when she continues to meet men that want nothing more than to sleep with her and use her. I learned how very painful it is to give your all to a person only to have that person belittle, berate, and disrespect you. You see, ladies, I believe that the Lord has allowed me to sample just a little of what many of you very special ladies have endured.

Through this book, I have been given the privilege of giving back to all of you some of the love, care, and acknowledgement that you have so graciously given me in my times of need, because without your help, this book would never have been written. Simply put, I don't feel that I can ever fully repay the debt.

With all of my love, thank you!

Kevin Waine

CONTENTS

K. Waine Golston, "Brown Sugar Pie" 1
Dedication To Melessa 3
Introduction 7

Chapter 1:
The Power in Loving a Black Woman-Sister ...15
    When We're Held by a Black Woman 17
    Love Is Also Respect 18
    When a Black Woman-Sister Makes Love to Us 20

Chapter 2:
The Strong Black Woman-Sister = A Strong Black Family (SBWS = SBF) 23
    The Foundation of the Black Family 23

Chapter 3:
The Spiritual Fire Keepers 29
    A Leadership Role Model 30
    The Look 30

Chapter 4:
Sisters Don't Take No Mess 35
    Some of Us Men Don't Count 36

Chapter 5:
The Changing Role of Black Women 41
    From Housekeeper to Entrepreneur and CEO . .41
    The Educated Black Woman-Sister 42
    Support of the Mind, Body, and Soul 43

Chapter 6:
50 Black Men Say Why They Love the Black Woman-Sister 47

Chapter 7:
Poems from My Heart 55

Chapter 8:
The Love of a Good Woman—
A True Gift Indeed! .75
    The Art of Listening 78

Chapter 9:
Just Hold On 81
    Keeping Your Faith and Hope 81

Chapter 10:
Conclusion 85
    A Message to All Women 87

Research Methodology 89
Brown Sugar Pie Recipe 91
A Very Special Thank You 93

Brown Sugar Pie

Brown Sugar Pie,
how so very pretty and tasty your are,
with your wonderful flavors of chocolate, toffee, coffee,
sweet cream, and all of your special flavors in between.
My lemon drop, my sugar stop,
Candy must be your
middle name
because your sweetness must be my weakness.
Brown Sugar Pie,
with the deep sweetness that you are,
you are both my sugar and spiritual spice and
all of the things that I like, naughty and nice.
You are truly a Brown Sugar Pie indeed!

Dedication

This book is dedicated to the memory of my wife, Melessa Golston, born August 19, 1957. She passed away from breast cancer on June 25, 1996. Melessa was a fantastic mother and wife, a true Black Woman-Sister. May my love warm her soul as her love surely warms mine.

This book is also dedicated to all of you wonderful Black Woman-Sisters out there; you have and will surely always be a blessing to the world. Thank you for your love, support, patience, kindness, strength, and most importantly your faith in God. May the good Lord's warm breath always be a soothing bubble bath for your soul.

I Was Truly Blessed

I do remember when we met.
We shared so many memories, you and I.
I felt your arms in mine as we lay side by side
    on the beach of life.
I tasted the sugar of your love and drank so many
    times.
I hear our laughter as we've grown together.
When you have walked
through the doors of life before me, I am relieved
    to find
that you held the door open for me so that I may
    pass through
with you.

        Thank you, Melessa.

Introduction

One of the primary reasons why I wrote this book after the death of my wife Melessa was to share with the world how very thankful I was that God blessed me with someone so loving and giving as Melessa. Melessa was a woman who possessed a great deal of quiet strength. Through her faith in the Lord, she had the ability during extremely stressful situations to be as calm as the still water of a mountain lake. During those same periods of stress, others would panic, but not Melessa. She would just say, "My faith is in the Lord." Melessa was also the kind of woman that would never say a negative word about anyone. She would often tell me that before she would say anything negative about someone she would rather say nothing at all. To put it simply, Melessa was a kind, gentle, caring-yet-strong Black Woman-Sister. In some ways she was stronger than me, and there was never a time when this Black Woman-Sister didn't have my back. She would always say to me, "I'm right here for you, babe." In addition, Melessa was special, and not only to our boys and me; she was special to everyone she knew. I was blessed to have had this woman choose me as her life partner. I know that she loved us and I believe that she knows that we loved her. I thank the good Lord for his blessing, and a Black Woman-Sister named Melessa Fay Golston, and for allowing me the privilege of loving and taking care of her, like she would have surely taken care of me. A true gift from God.

Secondly, there is no way to say it but to say it this way: "I love my Black Woman-Sisters." Let me explain what I mean by the term "Black Woman-Sister." The name Black Woman-Sister is a term of endearment that I have created that clearly shows completely what I believe a black woman is to the majority of black men. She is African; she is and always has been a woman of strength. She is my sister of guardianship in a spiritual sense. The Black Woman-Sister (or BWS for short) is all things positive and strong. My parents raised me to know that a Black Woman-Sister is a woman that you can truly understand and find in any shape, size, or flavor (skin tone). In other words, "little, short, or tall, as a black man I love them all." For far too long, America has tried to make our BWS's feel less than, simply because they typically don't look like Caucasian women. Well, to hell with that notion. I have personally talked to and surveyed over 2,000 black men who feel the same way that I do. We appreciate the hair, the hips, the lips, the toes, and the wide nose.

As black men, we love our fabulous black women, whether they are dark as the darkest chocolate or as light as cream and every shade in between, you are all ours. Again, for far too long, we as black men have let someone else dictate to us what was desirable and beautiful, and that too is outrageous. One friend of mine once told me of how he was sitting in the Los Angles Airport waiting for a flight when all of a sudden this stunning Black

Woman-Sister walked up to the ticket counter and started a conversation. His breath was taken away, all he could do was sit there and thank the Lord for being a black man who could appreciate such beauty and intellect.

As an appreciator and admirer of the Black Woman-Sister, I find that she is intelligent, elegant, and graceful under extreme stress and pressure, such as when she has to deal with the stress of working in hostile environment or when she has to routinely deal with a society that has historically treated her with prejudice and disrespect. Still, the BWS handles these types of situations with grace and finesse, all of the time knowing that she has to survive because she has a family to care for, particularly when she has to be the mother and father in a home where no man is present.

Now ladies, I can and do understand and most importantly appreciate the independent spirit that makes the Black Woman-Sister a fascinating lady to know. For example, the BWS can hold her own in any given social situation, such as when she has to have her car worked on and the mechanic assumes that he can rip her off by charging her for repairs that aren't need, or when he will ask to speak to her husband simply because she is a woman, and yet she still manages to hold her own. The Black Woman-Sister is truly an extremely capable woman. Another example would be the fact that she has the strength in her personality that enables her to stand firmly on her convictions, even if those convictions are politically unpopular.

One of the most intriguing qualities that I have found in our Black Woman-Sisters is that throughout our history, the Black Woman-Sister has always possessed an enormous amount of strength, loyalty, and understanding of herself, family, and the black man. The Black Woman-Sister has always been the foundation that supports most successful black men. Where would we be without them? The Black Woman-Sister has been and remains an important part of the black success story as a whole in America. Unfortunately, there are too many times when we as black men forget that the Black Woman-Sister is part of us all. As a father, I believe that this happens because we as black men are missing out on the fundamental teaching we would normally have received from our fathers. A black male child learns how to appreciate and treat the black woman by observing the actions of his father. If the father is not around or if he is around but is not a positive role model and is abusive to the black woman, the black male child may view this as an acceptable behavior and the negative actions are started all over again with the next generation. It is this writer's opinion that the BWS is the breast that feeds our souls and the arms that hold us, she is our great-grandmother, our mother, our sister, our wife, our girlfriend, and most importantly, she is our partner and mentor.

To our mothers, grandmothers, and great-grandmothers, we as black men thank you for scrubbing floors, cleaning toilets, enduring rape and disrespect, all for the sake of your family and your men. When we couldn't find work, you kept the family strong. Simply put, we thank you for your love, your struggle, and your never-ending strength—incredible.

Now please understand, I am not here to put down any other race of women. Quite the contrary, I and other black men are simply here to say loudly to our lovely, intelligent Black Woman-Sisters: we love you, we respect you, and as strong black men we WILL be here for you. We also truly thank you for continuing to allow us the opportunity to stand up and be black men through your daily love, understanding, faith, and support.

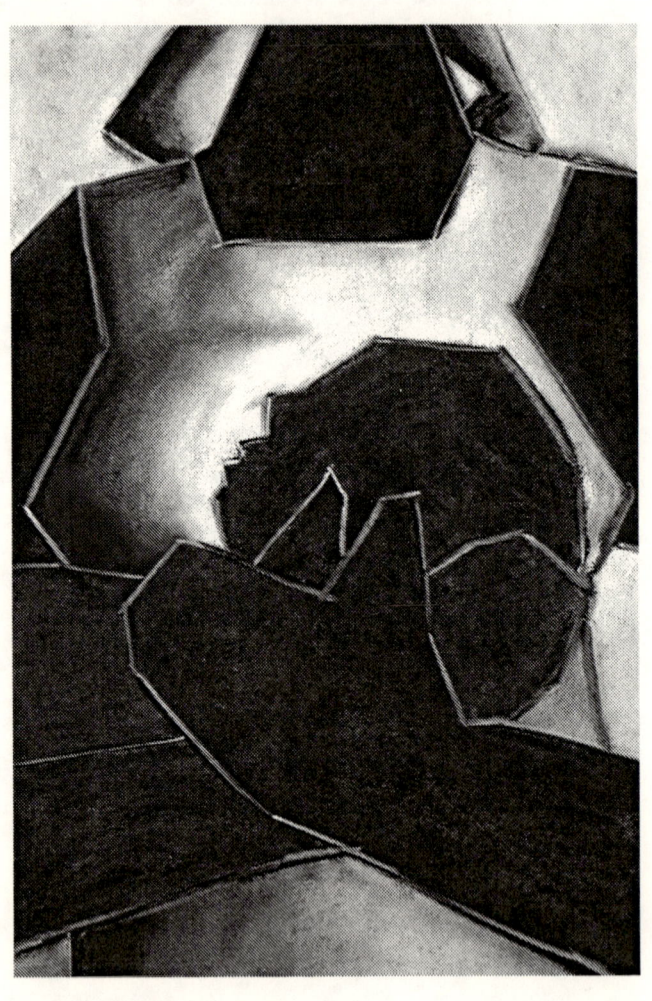

What Your Love Is

It is your Love that gives me purpose
to change and grow and learn.
It is your Love that guides me on this path
and helps me choose each turn.

It is your Love that gives me courage
to stand against my fears,
to open up my heart to you,
to let you see my tears.

It is your Love that gives me trust and hope
when little thing goes wrong.
When distance stands between us,
it is your Love that keeps me strong.

It is your Love that offers harmony
and a friendship that is true.
How wonderful that I can share
a love like this and give my
Love to you!

Chapter 1
The Power in Loving a Black Woman~Sister

When I began thinking about the power in loving a Black Woman-Sister, the first thought that came to mind, believe it or not, was a warm bubble bath. You see, when a black man is loved by a good Black Woman-Sister he feels loved, safe, and trusted. We get this warm feeling in our heart and soul, yes, very much like a warm bubble bath.

One thing we as black men are guilty of at times is failing to appreciate the true power of love that is ever-present in our Black Woman-Sisters. The kind of love that I am talking about is the love she has when you walk in from work and she knows just what you need, like massaging that little spot on your neck that seems to just melt that tension away. Or maybe it's when she says, "Baby, are you hungry?" and that's after she has worked her ass off all day herself.

There is something about the way a Black Woman-Sister supports us when we talk about our dreams, such as starting our own business, and she says something like "Well, baby, you know I support you." Now why can't more of our fellow black men treat and love our Black Woman-Sisters like that?

Personally speaking, ladies, I can truly say that when a Black Woman-Sister loves me, I sleep better, my health is better, I eat better, and hell—my bowels even function better. What can I say, there is a power in the love that a Black Woman-Sister gives us. Such as when you leave home for work in the morning, you feel like you can conquer the world. Sisters, you make us feel alive, you make us feel loved, needed, and most of all, you make us feel forgiven and understood. This is the power in loving a Black Woman-Sister.

Today, most black men understand that when we give you our unconditional love you are more than willing to give it back to us 100-fold. Sometimes I ask myself, "How are you able to do this?" particularly when we men at times act like asses. I have come to realize that this is as I like to put it "sister-love power" and I never cease to be amazed at how strong it is. Another example would be in the way you care for your children. My goodness, you seem to have an inexhaustible reservoir of love and understanding, and hugs are always at the ready.

For instance, what about when your kids at the last minute, I mean the night before at 8:30 p.m., decide to tell you that they need a lemon Jell-O sheet cake for 30 of their classmates? What do you do? By 9:15 p.m., you're in the kitchen baking that cake. Now make no mistake, you will have something to say about it, but it gets done, nevertheless. What about when you have to reach into your purse time after time and give your kids your last bit of money so that they can have a hot lunch at school that day? What about the many times when they were sick and you stayed up all night rubbing them down with Vicks Vapor Rub despite having to get up and go to work the next day because you needed that money to pay for rent, buy food, keep the lights on, and clothes on their back? And while at work, you still managed to call home or school throughout the day to see how your child was doing and if their fever had gone back up or whether they had eaten anything? Again, simply incredible!

Now I must share with you, ladies. As I am writing this, I can't help but think about my own mother and all of the wonderful Black Woman-Sisters that have loved me and fed my heart and soul, and it fills me with joy. The truth is that I was not prepared for how writing this would make me feel. Simply put, I find myself taken over by the wonderful feeling of love that I have for you all!

When We're Held By a Black Woman

When I am held by my black woman, her warm arms soothe my soul, when she touches me with her hands I feel with all my soul all of the work that God put into making her.

When she kisses me, her lips, they feel like a blazing furnace that warms me to my core. She heals me when I am weak, tired, or sick. She is and always will be the original chicken soup for mankind's soul and the needed sustenance for my heart. One taste of her dark Karo Syrup of love and I am forever addicted to her love, her strength and her kindness. How can I ever be any place but by her side? She is the only woman that can truly feed my mind, body, and soul. I am truly thankful for God's great gift, my pretty black woman.

Love is also respect

As a child, I was taught that the art of love is the science of respect. I was shown that we are unable to love one another without first showing each other respect. This rule can most certainly apply to our BWS's. My mother said to me countless times, "Treat your woman the way you would want a man to treat me."

The Black Woman-Sister is a very personal type of woman. She has a very sincere interest in others, particularly children and the elderly. She is very comfortable forming lasting and meaningful relationships with others. In other words, if you are a friend of hers, then you will have a friend for life. However, if for some reason she needs your help, the BWS will also expect you to be there for her, which is only fair.

For far too long I have seen a very disturbing trend. There is a movement towards open and blatant degradation and disrespect of our BWS's. I am saddened to say that I have seen the disrespect up close and personal through experiences with my wife and far too many other BWS's, for that matter. I recall my wife coming home many a day, telling me of how she had been repeatedly propositioned by her boss and how his actions made her feel. Initially, Melissa had not wanted to tell me about the incident due to the fact that she wanted to handle the matter in her own way since she needed the job. However, we decided that no job was worth being disrespected and, of course, the Lord would provide. I have also seen the disrespect of our BWS's on the streets, in the work place, and most of all in music videos. Most videos show our BWS's grabbing themselves and showing themselves in some of the most disrespectful ways that I have ever seen just to make a dollar. If as a black man, I say that I love my BWS's, then how can I condone or applaud all of those negative images? The bottom line is that I cannot.

Thank God, there is a segment of black men out here that do appreciate our BWS's. We don't approach them like sexual objects. We don't call them bitches, and we do respect them to the fullest. Yes, we are out here. Most importantly, there are many black men out here that refuse to sit by as our BWS's are berated, even by a small number of our own brothers, some of whom are still in the land of darkness. It is incumbent on all of us to guide them gently or forcefully to the light, but to the light they must go.

I would like say to all of you fantastic BWS's out there: respect begins at home; always remember that you are the descendants of queens. Without a doubt, you have the strength and the power of the ages. You gave birth to man and you are special in every way. With all of that said, just remember one thing, if you don't get anything else from this book get this, ALWAYS BE GOOD TO YOURSELF, love yourself first, respect yourself first. If you have someone in your life, whether they are personal or professional, demand respect. If you see a fellow BWS not being good to herself help her, lead her to the light, and the light shall also shine on all of us.

When a Black Woman~Sister Makes Love to Us

During a recent focus group of black men, I asked them to talk a little about the love and affection that comes from Black Woman-Sisters when they make love to us. The interesting fact is that almost immediately all the men present developed big smiles on their faces at that very thought. Let me try to put all of these opinions in a nutshell.

First, ladies, you are the unselfish lover personified. The fact is that it seems that you make love to us with every part of your being, heart, soul, mind, and last but certainly not least, your body. You see, as black men, we know that if you are loved, respected, appreciated, and shown that you are a priority in our lives, the love that comes from you is incredibly deep and enduring. Simply, ladies, you make us as men feel things that we can feel in no other aspect of our lives. We rush home to be with you and we call throughout the day just to hear your voice. Even our homies know who comes first in our lives. This is the power of being loved and loving a Black Woman-Sister.

Strength of a Black Woman

The strength of the Black Woman comes from God.
She holds that strength in her hands, like a gardener
holds fresh sod.

It comes from her mind, body, and soul,
This place that I speak of is mankind's spiritual
mold.

The strength of a Black Woman is steel, brick, and
strong rope,
And the many gifts that she has always give us hope.

The strength of a Black Woman helps us all to heal,
The strength of the Black Woman gives her that
incredible will.

Chapter 2
The Strong Black Woman~Sister = A Strong Black Family

The Foundation of the Black Family

The Black Woman-Sister has always remained the focal point of the black family and her community. Despite facing great obstacles, she has managed to maintain a climate of stability for both herself and her family. Take for example, Dr. Martin Luther King, Jr.. While Dr. King was out fighting for a better world, his Black Woman-Sister was busy maintaining the home front. Not only was Mrs. Coretta Scott King caring for their children, she was also active in the community and church, all the while supporting her husband. I am sure that when Dr. King arrived back home, she was even there to help him recharge, so that he could fight another day. What a phenomenal Black Woman-Sister.

When General Colin Powell was climbing the ladder of success within the U. S. Army, he knew, I'm sure, that his Black Woman-Sister was his best and strongest partner and friend. What I am attempting to illustrate here, as a black man in

America, is that the BWS has always been there for her family and community. Put another way, as with any ship, in life, the Black Woman-Sister is sometimes the captain, sometimes the engine or at times the rudder, but she always manages to keep her family going in the right direction.

How many times have we seen celebrities or professional athletes attribute their success to their mother, wife, or grandmother? How many times have we seen someone wave to the camera and say "Hi, mom"? In June of 2001, I interviewed a group of African-American Vietnam war vets and I asked them, when one of their fellow soldiers had been hit or was dying, what were the last words many would say? Their overwhelming response was that those black soldiers would say, "Tell my mother I love her." Now that is profound, to say the least. Again, what I am illustrating here is that a strong black woman equals a strong black family or a least a far greater chance of being one, and her kids will never forget her love and sacrifice.

For the last nine years, I have had the privilege of working as a volunteer crisis hotline counselor for the Center for Battered and Abused Women. This non-profit organization's primary mission is to help battered women survive after leaving very abusive situations. Subsequently, I witnessed so many times the BWS's ability to survive in situations, many times with children, where others did not.

I witnessed, for example, BWS's in homeless shelters maintaining their commitment to church and their children by keeping their kids in school, off of the streets, clean, healthy, and fed. Most importantly, they gave their children a sense of stability in a very unstable situation by showing them a deep degree of love and support despite not having any real support except from church, friends, and of course, the Lord.

Another example that comes to my mind is from my own mother. My mother was a nurse in Los Angeles, California. I remember times when my mother would bring home left over food from the hospital kitchen that a friend would wrap up and leave under the bushes for her to pick up after work. Again, this BWS, my mother, had a deep drive to provide for her kids, a trait I still find in the Black Woman-Sister today.

Do you remember when your mother would say something like: "Before I will let my babies go hungry, I will go out on the streets." I sure do, and guess what? I have not met a BWS yet that didn't mean it. You see, you BWS's have what we would call when I was in the Army, "Uncommon Valor." Simply incredible! All I can say is this, ladies, you are special as hell. You warm our souls in so many, many ways, and if you ever forget, just email me and I will tell you again!

My Ebony Angel

She has come to me in my dreams and prayers.
Because of my faith in the Lord, I knew she'd
Be there.

My ebony angel's loving touch, smile, and voice
Assure my soul that the Lord has made the right choice.

She is my dream come true; I have truly been so blessed.
She gives me the gentle, deep love I need
that allows my soul to rest.

I have awakened again,
She's now gone,
I now must pray for sleep once more
So that she won't be away for long.

Chapter 3
The Spiritual Fire Keepers

Let's talk about the commitment of Black Woman-Sisters to our religious roots. As a child, I can remember many times when I was too lazy to get up and go to church. My mother would say, "Kevin, you are going to get your butt up. You are going to church." And yes, off to the Lord's house we would go. As mothers, you are the ones that established many of our fundamental spiritual rules and boundaries that we as adults continue to live by to this day. You have given us the fundamental love and structure needed to become the women, men, and parents that we are today.

I remember times when I would get into trouble at school (which was fairly often) and my mother would go to the school, angry to no end for having to get off work in order to deal with some mess that I had gotten myself into. But despite her anger with me, she would pull me to the side and say, "You need to tell me the truth so that I will know how to fight for you, and if you lie to me, I can't fight for you." Of course, when we got home, I would get my ass beat, but in public, she was always there for me, even when I was in the wrong, yet another example of what a black mother will do for her children. The BWS has always been the steel that supports our emotional skyscraper. Always remember that she will be there for you in your time of need, but beware, she may just tell your ass off when you get home.

A Leadership Role Model

Simply put, the Black Woman-Sister has been unsurpassed by her ability to do the impossible when it comes to her family. She will work all day or all night long and then come home to cook, help with homework, and clean the house, and still have the energy to whip some ass if you had not done what she had asked when she called from work to check on you. Despite the enormously exhausting pace, the BWS will still have time to make sure that her family feels the hands of love that come from her heart.

The Look

Do you remember THE LOOK? The "look" was a facial expression your mother would give you as a child, when you were acting up—especially in public. She would stare at you with those piercing eyes and you just knew that your ass was in deep, deep, deep trouble. All you could do, if you had any sense, I mean any sense at all, was melt into the floor or corner and come correct, and hope the good Lord would smile on you and cause your mother to get a sudden, severe case of amnesia so you wouldn't get your ass beat when you got back home.

What about when you were a child and your mother would catch you doing something wrong? She would call you by your first, middle, and last name and again you knew that she was damn dead serious and again your ass just knew that you where in deep, deep, deep trouble. This kind of discipline and structure is what our mothers and Black Woman-Sisters have given us, and thank God they did!

When the Black Woman-Sister is one of the breadwinners, or the only breadwinner, she is willing to do whatever it takes to provide for her family, and I do mean whatever it takes to provide for her family. She is repeatedly abused and misused by her employers. The Black Woman-Sister will, for the sake of her family, especially her kids, put up with things on the job that would make a lesser woman try to leave this world. I have seen many Black Woman-Sisters working for ten and fifteen or more days straight, ten to twelve hours a day, and still managing to make their children's performances, football games, or parent-teacher conferences, in addition to making sure that all of their children's homework was completed on time. Again, where would we be without her? The Black Woman-Sister assumes a leadership position every time she gets out of bed. Now that is tremendous.

A Black Woman's Prayer of Faith

If I can endure for this moment,
whatever is happening to me.
No matter how heavy my heart,
or how dark the moment may be.
If I can but keep on believing
in the Lord and
what I know in my heart to be true.
This rain will fade into morning,
and with this dawns a new day of
faith in my God.

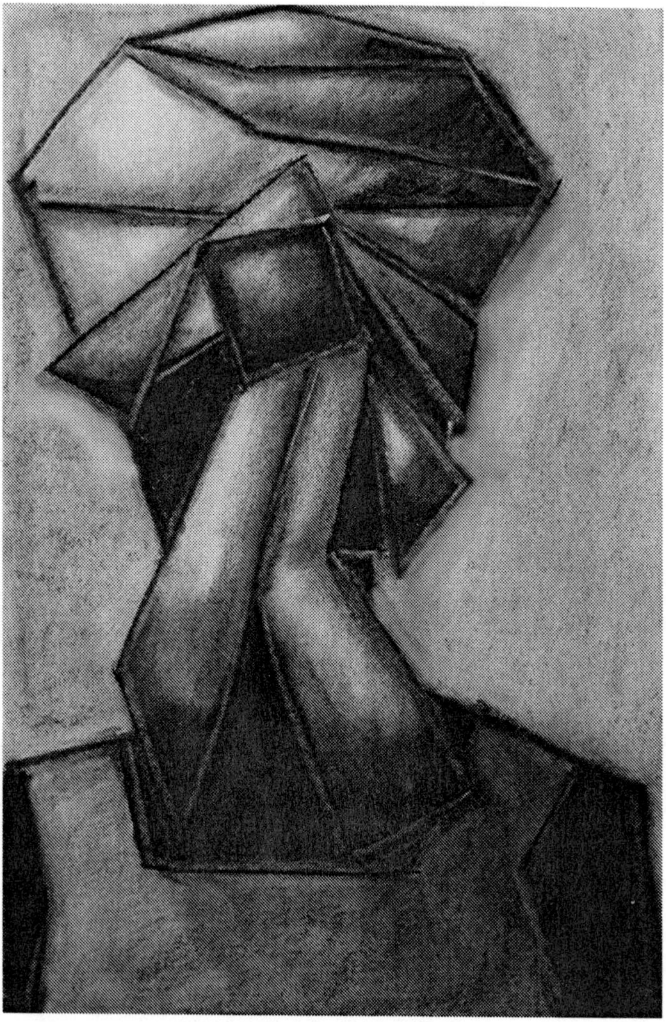

Chapter 4
Sisters Don't Take No Mess

Throughout our history, the BWS has never been one for not speaking her mind and making her feelings known. The BWS will tell you directly what she feels. Whether you are a man, woman, or child, you will never have any doubt about where you stand with her. If you treat her with a high degree of respect and appreciation, she will give you that same high degree of respect without fail. As one survey respondent said about his wife of 22 years, "A black woman will tell you where to go and how to get there and she will give you tremendous love, too."

Now for those of you who are women of another race or ethnic group, please don't misunderstand the message here; every woman of any race will vocalize her feelings when pushed long and hard enough. But it is generally believed by most black men surveyed that a BWS won't let you go too far with out saying something to you about it.

The truth is that I find it a great honor and privilege to be able to sit down and convey in this humble book our true feelings to all of you fabulous ladies. You see, ladies, there are times when we as men find it rather difficult to admit that much of the strength we posses is a result of the strength and faith that you have in us. We sometimes find it difficult just to say two words to you. Those two words are THANK YOU.

Some of Us Men Don't Count

I'm sure it will shock you to know that many black men feel that you should, from time-to-time, say to yourself, "Some of you men don't count." Well, it's true; some of us men don't count. To all of you ladies and men out there, please understand what I am saying. If you meet a man and he doesn't respect you, or he wants to criticize you in a manner that is non-constructive, or you find him being unfaithful and a liar, or he hits you or calls you names your parents never gave you—kick his ass to the curb so hard that he bounces up off the sidewalk, say to yourself "He doesn't count," and move on.

You see, ladies, a good man will respect and listen to you by treating you as a friend first, a partner second, and a lover third. A good man will empower you by helping and encouraging you to empower yourself at all times. He won't always insist that things go his way. Ladies, a good man will help with the kids, he will share in the cooking and cleaning, and he won't ask you to make love when he knows that you're not feeling well just to get his. He will treat you in a kind, loving, and gentle way, and yes ladies, he won't ask you to...if he won't do the same for you. Finally, a good man will put the Lord, his wife and kids, and honor first. He will be the provider and protector of his family, even if that means giving his life in order to do so.

The Greatness of Black

I know that there will be men out there who will read t[his and say all I'm] doing is bashing men. Simply p[ut, I'm not. On the] other hand, let's be very, very [honest about the] current state of affairs being w[...in the black] community, each and every black [man needs to take it] upon himself to raise the bar of th[e treatment of black] ladies just a little bit, and what's [wrong with that] anyway? That means go back home, [get rid of the] woman on the side if you have one (because she isn't worth a damn anyway), bring your entire check home, and for goodness sake, don't eyeball sports all day; try spending more time with your wife and family.

However, ladies, until we do, you just continue to be good to yourself and keep holding out for the good ones and stay away from the pretty Ricky's, because they aren't worth a damn either. Just think of the good ones, because we are out here. Remember this, until you find a good man, keep this book and whenever you feel down or losing hope, know that I will be with you to encourage you and remind you that you are loved and supported and special.

Kevin Waine

Dear Brown Sugar Sisters

We think of you often,
We miss you when you're not around.
Do you know things aren't the same
Since you've been gone?
Please believe in us again.
We miss you dearly.
We've been thinking about Sugar.
With all our love
Sincerely,
Black Men

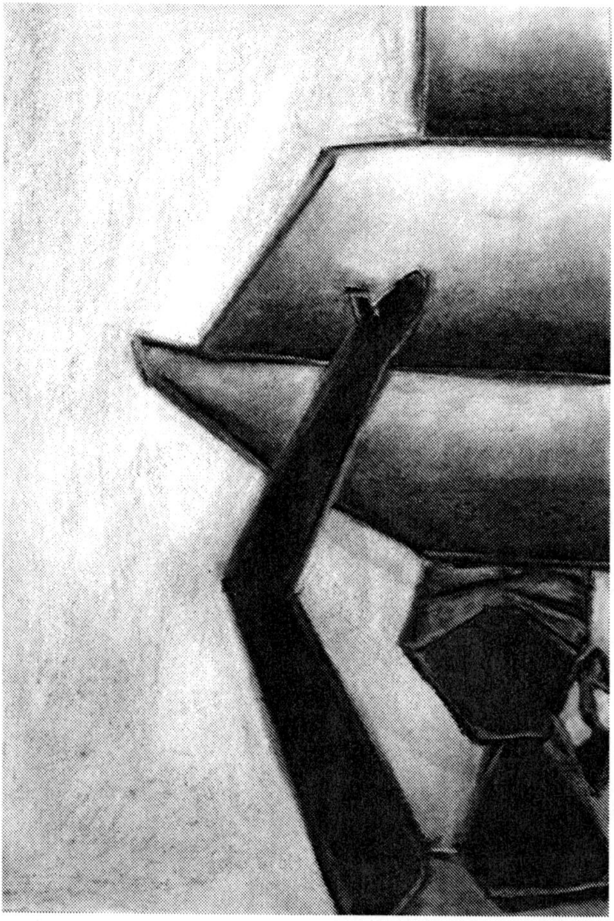

Chapter 5
The Changing Role of Black Woman~Sisters

From House Keeper to Entrepreneur to CEO

During the time of slavery, the BWS was relegated to the role of housekeeper or maid. Despite the fact that she has been a very capable and intelligent person, the BWS has had to swallow her pride and accept employment in some of the most degrading positions known, all the time keeping and instilling in her family the inner belief that you must not let anyone stop you from living your dreams and obtaining an education.

Some of our greatest leaders were influenced and supported by the BWS. As time began to slowly, and I mean slowly, change in America, the role of black women also began to change slowly. She had a few more options other than cleaning someone's toilet or scrubbing Miss Daisy's floor. She could become a doctor (like Rebecca Lee Crumpler, born 1833, the first BWS to earn a medical degree, The New England Female Medical College in Boston), or a teacher (like Mary Jane Patterson, born 1840, the first BWS to earn a B.A. degree and teach, Oberlin College in Oberlin, Ohio), or an entrepreneur (such as Madam C. J.

Walker aka Sarah Breedlove, born 1867, the first BWS millionaire, who created a successful line of black hair care products). No matter what other jobs or education the BWS could obtain, she has always remained true to her primary loves: her family and God. Somehow, the BWS manages to do it all.

Just imagine, if you will, a place and time were the BWS didn't play such a critical role in our very survival. If you think that the black community has problems now, just imagine if our mothers hadn't left a porch light on at night for her daughter who was out late with her friends, or told that daughter that the dress she was about to wear was way too short, and oh yes, you had better be home by midnight...just imagine our lives without her. The truth is, I don't want to imagine such a scenario. Isn't it ironic that despite all of the disrespect and criticism and negative images that the BWS has had to endure, American society is now attempting to copy her, as seen by the new interest in larger lips and rounder hips, or the so-called new hairstyles called corn rolls or French braids, the list goes on and on. Fortunately, the essence of the BWS can't be emulated through collagen shots, breast enlargements, or braids: it's a black soulful thing.

The Educated Black Woman~Sister

The New Educated Diva is a woman who has firmly determined that the way to financial independence is through the doors of academia, and becoming completely self-sufficient. The new educated BSW is really not new at all to education. In fact, despite vast institutional racism, the BWS has managed to maintain a foothold in the doors of higher learning. It is the opinion of this writer that the BWS was raised knowing that the only true way to escape poverty was to obtain a good education. Generally speaking, the BWS knew that she was not going to be offered very many opportunities to get on with the phone company or utility company and other positions like them.

The Black Woman-Sister, by educating herself, has emerged as a potent economic and political force to behold, and I am so thankful to be alive to see it. This has also helped her to become a more self-aware and secure woman. In the months of February, March, and April of 2001, I asked over 2,000 Black Women-Sisters, "What is your most important goal over the next 24 to 48 months?" Not to my surprise, 83 percent of the women surveyed said that they would like to either obtain or complete their education. By comparison, after surveying 2,053 black men, only 47 percent listed education as their primary goal over the next 24 to 48 months.

It is important to note that the black woman appears to view education somewhat differently than does the black man in general. The Black Woman-Sister sees education as a means of obtaining personal and financial security in a world that has, to a significant degree, always been hostile her.

Support of The Mind, Body and Soul

By now, you have probably come to the conclusion that it is the opinion of this writer that the

BWS is some kind of special woman, and she is. The main purpose here is not to build her up as an extraordinary woman, which she is: the purpose is to also show that a BWS is able to accomplish her objectives and survive due to her sheer will and the support she receives from a wide array of sources. Her parents may help her care for the smaller children when the BWS has to work late or go to class at night. She may have support from close girlfriends who may encourage her to stay on track and remain positive by never letting her lose hope. The BWS also has the faith of her God, which sustains her during both challenging and good times.

The church is another excellent source of support. It is a place where she can spiritually recharge. Unfortunately, the BWS can't always rely on the support of her black man. The truth is that all too often, the black male has left the household, leaving the BWS the responsibility of raising the family, and this must stop now. Nevertheless, despite enormous mental anguish, and in addition to rather low-paying jobs, the BWS still keeps moving ahead and that is phenomenal, to say the least.

Finally, ladies, let me say this. If you are reading this part of the book, I certainly hope that by now you are feeling very warm and loved because the way you affect us is so necessary.

I want your spiritual palate to begin to taste the sugar sweet fruit of our love and admiration because simply put, ladies, you have had fare too much bitter, and sweet love is the only sensation I want you to feel, so if you do well, then mission accomplished!

I Love A Classy Black Woman

I love a classy black woman because of her strength,
style, and finesse.

I love a classy black woman because I know that I
have the
best.

I love a classy black woman in every shape and size,
It's easy to spot a classy black woman
Because you can see it in their
Loving eyes.

The classy black woman makes me feel good and
strong
It's a shame the classy black woman has been
disrespected by man for far so damned long.

So when you see a black woman and you look into
her eyes
Just make sure that you bring your "A" game
Because that is where Intelligence lies.

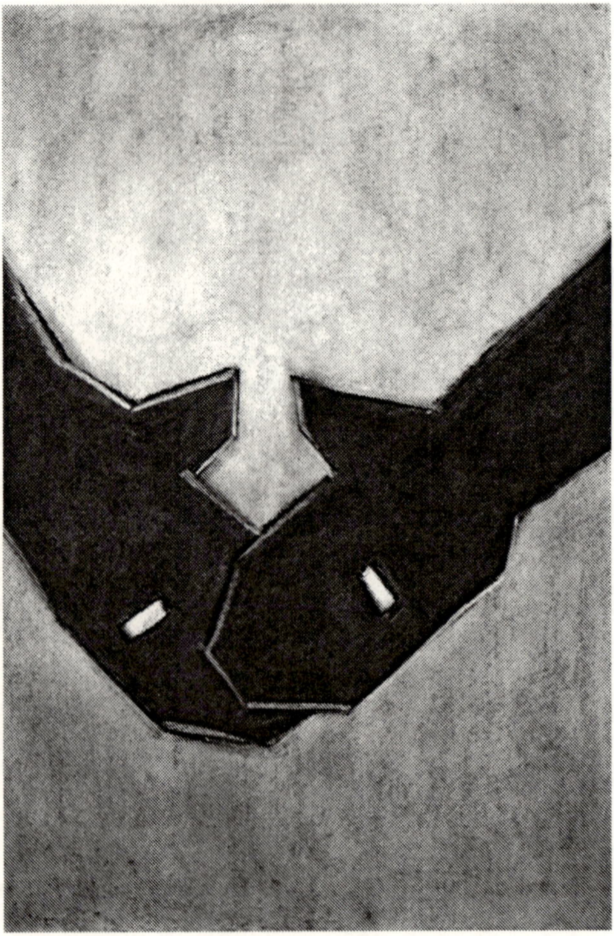

Chapter 6
50 Black Men Say Why They Love Sisters

Due to the high percentage of surveys returned and limited space, I have elected to only include fifty of the responses, instead of the more than 2000 loving opinions on why we love sisters. I certainly hope that you will get a good feel for what we are thinking out here.

So you would like to know what 50 black men said about why we love you? Well, here it is. Enjoy!

#1.   Thomas H., San Diego, CA
A black woman is sweeter than chocolate milk, as strong as ebony and more beautiful than the cradle of the earth.

#2.   Reginald M., Denver, CO
I love my sister because she has style and spirit, and that's just what I need.

#3.   Mark T., Washington, D.C.
The black woman has the patience with her kids that you don't see everyday.

#4.   Mark B., Key West, FL
She has the focus and determination that I find admirable.

#5.   Tony L., Detroit, MI.
After you have gotten you butt kicked out there in the world, a sister will let you know it's still OK.

#6.   Henry W., Carson, CA
I love the black woman because she has had similar experiences.

#7.   James R., Odessa, TX
A black woman, if she is in your corner, will always have your back.

#8.   Mark J., Carlsbad, CA
What can I say? Her beauty, her background, her faith in God.

#9.   Damask G., San Diego, CA
The black woman is my mother, a role model; she is my heart.

#10.   David G., Colorado Springs, CO
Sisters are my friends, my wife, and my guide.

#11.   Mike S., Charlotte, NC
When I see a sister, I see a lady of strength.

#12.   Randall W., Queens, NY
My mother is one of the finest black women I know; she showed me love and discipline.

#13.   Teulae S., Las Vegas, NV
She is trusting and a good friend when you need one.

#14.   Tony S., New Orleans, LA
A black woman is like a good pot of gumbo, with all the right things in her.

#15.   James R., Gulf Port, MS
Similarities of values and ideologies.

#16.   Trent R., Phoenix, AZ
All of the sisters that I have known are good role models and have a strong will.

#17.   Randy J., Seattle, WA
The black sister is assertive and knows what she wants.

#18.   Tommy L., Colorado Springs, CO
She give the black man support and she gives me purpose.

#19.   Laroy A., Saint Louis, MO
I love her dark complexion, her sex appeal, and her strength.

#20.   Robert R., Albany, NY
She gives me pride in myself.

#21.   Von W., Anderson, SC
What can I say; she is just good to me.

#22.   Tomas D., Bakersfield, CA
Her looks, attitude, and encouragement.

#23.   Wes P., Hillsboro, OH
Just everything; her drive, and the way she drives me.

#24.   Steven K., Hollywood, FL
The average sister is grounded in God and rooted in Christ. I like that.

#25.   Herman W., San Diego, CA
She has good family values.

#26.   William S., New York, NY
The black woman is a very beautiful woman. God knew what He was doing.

#27.   David K., High Point, NC
A black woman never gives up.

#28.   Darrious S., Kemp, TX
I can relate to them very well, they are part of my heart.

#29.   Clint W., Palm Springs, CA
A sister can be very independent, protective, and driven.

#30.   Nicholas E., Pasadena, TX
I love the black woman because she is there on the front of this war of genocide against us.

#31.   Mark J., Norfolk, VA
The sister is reliable as a Swiss watch, as warm as a blanket, and my friend.

#32.   John G., Oakland, CA
When I was down, she held me up, when I was lost, she helped me find my way—she's a black woman, thank God.

#33. Bobby W., Portsmouth, OH
From the lesser to the greater of them, they are all queens.

#34. Cleo R., Galt, CA
A black woman has morals and values. She motivates me in so many ways.

#35. Ken T., Roanoke, VA
If I had three wishes, I would wish for a Jaguar, a custom home, and a sister.

#36. Rodger L., Charleston, SC
I love her personality and the fact that she is down to earth.

#37. Ben D., Newport, OR
Sisters are deep.

#38. John S., Los Angeles, CA
If you are a decent man, a black woman will accept you as you are.

#39. Henry A. Dallas, TX
A sister is beautiful, intelligent, and a partner.

#40. Andrew K. Jackson, TN
The black woman has a rich history that I am personally proud of.

#41. Don S., Washington, D.C.
I just want the kind of love that my father had, and that love was with a black woman.

#42. Paul H. Dallas, TX
With a good black woman, anything is possible.

#43.   Vernon S., Miami, FL
Black woman comes in many shapes and sizes and I like all of them.

#44.   Neil K., New Orleans, LA
I like the way a sister speaks her mind.

#45.   Jaime N., Scripps Ranch, CA
My mother is one of the finest black woman I know; she taught me the difference between right and wrong.

#46.   Cliff W., San Antonio, TX
Black woman is a joy to be around. Being without them is like food without seasoning.

#47.   Chris C., Gulfport, MS.
I don't know where I would be without the black woman. She has given me life, she has given me hope. She has been there for me when I was alone. She is hope eternal.

#48.   Alan H., Albuquerque, MN
The black woman has been one of the most enduring females in the world, and she keeps enduring with her head up.

#49.   Charles H., Chicago, CA
How do I spell Great? B.L.A.C.K. W.O.M.A.N.

...Last but not least, yours truly.

#50.   Kevin Waine, San Diego, CA
The Black Woman-Sister is the North Star in my universe. She gives me a warm feeling inside, a feeling that says we can make it together. She is my mother,

who never let me miss a meal or be without a safe place to lay my head. She was my wife, who sat with me when I was sick. Simply put, the Black Woman-Sister is my everything and I am the man I am because of her. Thank God she is!

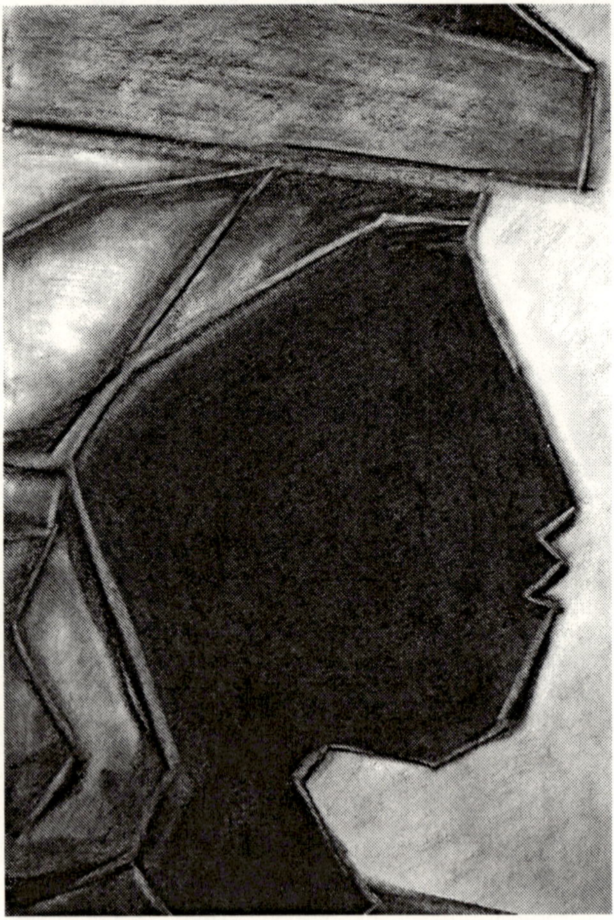

Chapter 7
Poems From My Heart

Oh Chocolate Girl

Oh
Chocolate girl,
Sweet and tasty you are.
Your flavors melt my soul,
Your smile is my guiding star.

The
Sugar of your heart
Reminds me of hot marshmallow
Cocoa on a winter's day,
Sipping you slowly so
That your flavor will never
Fade away.

Oh
Chocolate girl,
How I love all of the
Flavors that you are.
The taste of you will
Forever linger on my tongue
As a sweet and rich Chocolate bar.

A Prayer for the Black Woman-Sister

Oh dear Lord God,
I humbly come before you,
thanking you for the wonderful gift of
a black woman.
Father, I respectfully ask that you keep
them strong.
Father, I ask that your hand will always be with
them.
Finally, Father, I humbly ask that
you will bless the men in their lives with
wisdom, love, and patience so
that we may become better men, husbands, and
fathers.
Father, I ask this in your name,
Lord God.
Amen!

The Beauty of a Black Woman

The beauty of a black woman is not in the clothes she wears,
Or the size she is or the length of her hair.
The beauty of a black woman must be seen from
Her eyes, because that is the doorway to her
Heart, the place where love lies.
The beauty of a black woman is not in the
Material goods she holds,
But the true beauty of a black woman is reflected in her soul.

The love & beauty of a good woman, a true gift indeed!

A Mother's Love

She carried us for nine months in that place within.
It's that place I'm talking about
Where life begins.

She loved and cared for us and kept us fed,
And gave us that last kiss and hug at the end of the day,
As she tucked us into bed.

What can I tell you about a Mother's love?
It is something that truly comes from the
merciful God above.

No one will love you like your Mother will,
Let someone mess with one of hers and she will kill.

The looks she gave you when she didn't like something you'd done.
The love that she gives us, we know, can only come from one.

As I Gaze Into Your Eyes

As I gaze into twin pools of warmth
bright and sparkling,
I see something indescribable,
something I can't quite put my finger on.

Your twin pools blazing and brilliant
make all your sweetness
and your compassion
crystal clear.

Your twin pools shimmering and glimmering
show how sweet, sensitive, caring, kind,
funny, and friendly you are.

Your twin pools, so animated and intense, have
help me to share your love of life,
your life of love.

As I gaze into the twin pools of warmth,
I see the sweetest person I've met in a long time, and
I recognize a sincere and honest woman who will
never be replaced, and
I realize you are so special because
when I look into your eyes
I realize that I have witnessed a miracle, the making of
a friend.

If I Lost My Black Woman

If I lost my black woman, where would I be?

How would I deal with the loss of someone so
Dear to me?

If I lost my black woman, how would I cope
After I have lost all
Hope?

If I lost my black woman,
The greatest loss of all would
Be the loss of her love, a gift from
The merciful God above.

The Candlelight and You

As the candle flickers in the night
Your eyes reflect its light
Like perfect diamonds,
And I say to myself, How can
This be?

As the candles light your
Essence in that warm womb
Called a bubble bath, and
I'm gently washing your
Back, I say to myself,
How can this be?

As the warm candle wax
Lovingly drips over your body
I once again asked myself,
How can this be?

And God answered
"Because I have given
You the very special gift
Of a black woman's
Love."

Now I know how this
Can be.

My Saving Grace

The brown hue of your skin
Is where all time begins.
It is your love that takes me
to a place between time and
space when I am with you my
very special black woman,
my saving grace.

Dreaming Of You

At night in my depth of sleep
I dream of you,
my cinnamon girl.
I am holding you,
I am loving you,
I am wanting you,
And with each of your
Caresses it is then that
I truly know that I am
Being touched by a
Messenger of God.

When She Touches Me

When she touches me,
I feel the thrill and chill
knowing that the love she is
Giving is her will.

When she touches me,
there is a warmth
that emanates from
her soul that
will most certainly never
grow cold.

When a black woman touches me,
All of my senses come alive
And my heart begins to
Thrive and I
Know that I'm home,
And I am blessed to have a
Black woman in my life.

It's All Good

The memory of your eyes
Can make any man feel warm,
It's all good!

The bright sun of your smile
Shows your heart,
It's all good!

The soft touch of your hand,
It's all good!

The gentle hue of your cinnamon brown skin,
It's all good!

The special black woman that
You are,
It's all, all good!

"I've Never Been Here Before"

She walked into that coffee shop,
My God, she instantly took my heart.

As she looked at me, our eyes met each other in
love dance with her smile playing a gentle song,
putting me in a trance.
"I've never been here before," I say.

I tried not to seem so obvious,
But my heat betrayed me again and again
because "I've never been here before."

As I looked around the room quickly, quietly
like a little boy that has found a new $100 bill,
all the time praying that no other man
will see this rare diamond because,
"I've never been here before,"

As I say a prayer to God asking for the right words
to say to her, I say to myself one last time,
"I've never been here before, help me Lord."

A Taste and Smell of Chocolate

She's got that loving thing going on,
Her movements play a gentle sexy song.

The visual taste of chocolate satiates my desires,
Just the touch of her lights my
Spiritual fire.

How can I possibly thank God enough for such a
wonderful gift?
He has blessed me with the taste of chocolate,
This black woman has soothed my soul with just one
whiff.

My Heart to Your Heart

The first time I saw her, I could not find my breath,
she made me feel free in ways that I can't forget.
When I held her for the first time she helped my soul,
this is a feeling I will have and keep as I grow old.

When I smell her sweet perfume, it puts me in a
trance,
I can only say that this woman took my heart
with one glance.

She makes me want to thank the Lord for making my
dream come true. I have given my promise to this
Beautiful Nubian woman to always be true.

She is a woman that I pray I never lose,
because if I lost this black woman out of my life
I would surely lose.
Oh Lord, how can I love her better and be the one she
needs?
I promise, Lord, to respect her and always try to
please.

A Black Man's Best Friend

As a black woman and the lady in my life, you are my very best friend.
You have continued to love me throughout the changing seasons of our relationship.
When I'm not the most understanding, you are patient.
When I don't listen as much as I should, you will repeat what you have said.
When my temper is too short, you are calming.
Despite my faults, you are always there ready to lend an understanding ear
or a reassuring touch and anything else I may need.
For all the beautiful things you do...I love you.

Always Remember Her

Remember to make time before it passes by.
Remember that care is sometimes just being there.
Remember to hold her heart softly with both hands.
Remember that is the strength of a true loving man.

Some Say

Some say they have arrived when they have an expensive car.
Some say they have arrived when they have a large home.
Some say they have arrived when they have fancy clothes.
But I say I have arrived when I have a black woman by my side.

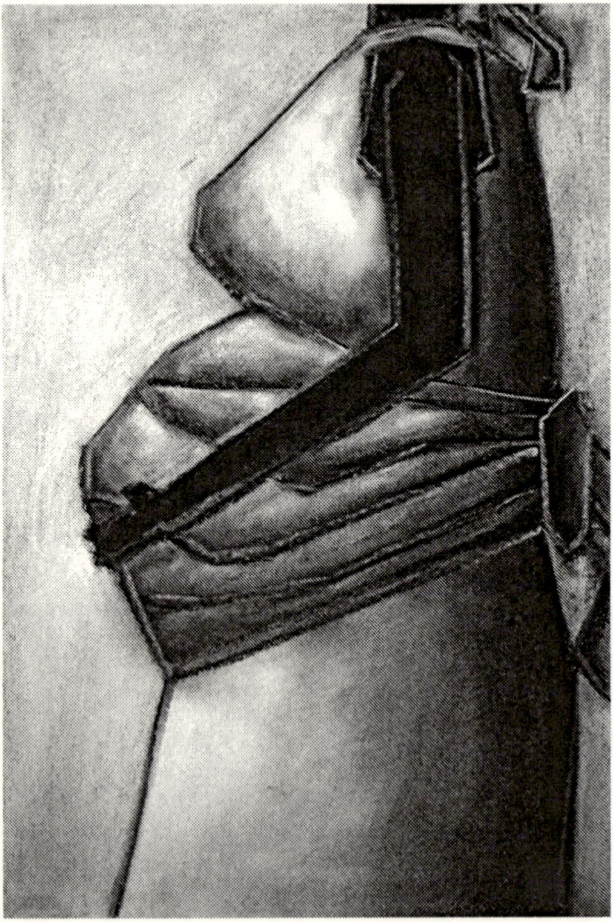

Your Love

I have never known a woman like you except in my dreams.
The gentle way that you listen.
The gentle way that you touch.
The way that you allow me to please you, makes me fear
that you are a dream and that when I will awake you'll be gone.
But with a gentle kiss you continue to reassure me that you aren't a dream, just very special blessing.
May God never let me forget his gentle blessings....

Chapter 8
The Love of A Good Woman~ A True Gift Indeed!

Even though this book is written for my very special Black Woman-Sisters, I want to say a few words to my fellow black men. You know, guys, sometimes we as men take for granted the love of a good woman. At times we feel that because there are so many women out there, we can take the one we have for granted by associating quantity with quality and it's just not necessarily true. I am here to say to you that "good" in a woman has nothing to do with external beauty, or how much she earns, or what she wears, how long her hair is, or how thin she is. A good woman is someone that loves you when you make dumb-ass mistakes, supports your dreams, and is there when you feel down. A good woman is someone that you know will always be there for you when no one else is. Fellas, have you ever had a so-called good friend that always wanted to come over, and you thought he was a true friend until one day while you are at work he just pops up at your house in an attempt to hit on your lady? However, your fantastic lady respectfully yet directly puts him in his place by stopping him in his pathetic tracks and cussing him out if need be. Then, in that quiet time as you both are going to bed, she tells you something like, "You know baby, John isn't your friend." That is what I mean by a good woman. She holds her own by respecting herself and you, too. Guys, just do me one favor: if you are blessed enough to have a good woman like that, listen to her when she warns you about John.

Now I know, guys, right about now you may be saying to yourself, " I know what a good woman is." I want to give you my opinion of what I think is necessary for us as men to appreciate a good woman. You see, a good man will always appreciate a good woman. When we as men appreciate a good woman, our tone when we speak to her will be loving and calm, our heart will be open, our touch will be gentle, our words will be kind.

Now there will be times when we don't agree with something that she says or does, but when we truly appreciate and love a good woman, we don't worry about those little things. Instead, what you do is you take her in your arms and look her in the eyes and you tell her how much you appreciate her and you thank the good Lord for allowing you to be in her life and for having her in yours.

Sometimes we as men don't truly appreciate what we have until we lose it. I my case, I felt that I was a pretty good husband and friend to my wife by being supportive and loving. But one of the things that I realized after my wife Melessa passed away was that with a good woman, we don't realize the many things that they do for us, our kids, or for others, for that matter. We don't realize how much they do until they're gone, and guys, when they're gone, everything that they did stops.

Now I want to explain precisely what I mean when I say, "gone." This could mean death, divorce, or the end of a relationship; they are all the same. They're out of your life. You begin to miss the little things, like the smell of her perfume or the spot that she keeps warm on her side of the bed. You begin to miss the gentle loving touch of her hand on yours. You miss the way she cooked that fried chicken or gumbo. Maybe it was the way she would ask you "Hey baby, do you want me to wash your back?" So what I am saying to you, guys, is that if you are blessed to have a good woman in your life...someone that you know loves you even when you mess up...someone you know you can trust and trust you...someone you will love and appreciate...I want to say one more time, if you're blessed enough to have that type of woman in your life, hold on to her, love her, soak her up with a very large emotional sponge, speak to her in a kind, gentle fashion, and treat her in a Godly way, because take it from me, you have a true gift on your hands.

Finally, guys, there are times when we complain to our so-called friends and we sometimes say things in passing about our women that just aren't respectful. I want to tell you, from one man to another, that's not right at all. We don't complain when they are laying on a table with their legs open to the world giving birth to our children, and we certainly don't complain when we want them to make love to us. You see, again, I believe that when the Lord blesses us with his gifts, such as a good woman, you had better respect, appreciate, and love her, or the Lord will take her away. We as men must in thought; word, and deed rejoice in the knowledge that we have a good woman and have been truly blessed.

The Art of Listening

Some times we have a tendency to forget what our black woman needs every now and then. There are times when your lady comes home and she wants to tell you how her day was. She wants to share with you, the man in her life, her hopes and pains. All your lady, partner, and friend is asking for is your undivided attention. What she doesn't want is for you to pay more attention to the TV than you do her. She doesn't need for you to criticize her by say she should have said this or done that. Fellas, your woman just wants you to listen and understand. She wants you to tell her that you love her and that she's very special to you and others and you truly support her. Finally, she needs to know that one of the many things that you love about her is her mental and spiritual strength and that you have complete faith in her in whatever she is doing.

As a conflict management consultant, I feel that the art of listening is a skill that is learned. However, this society does not prize a man that listens. Personally, I was taught to listen by my wife Melessa. She was willing to teach me and I was willing to learn. You see, listening is not just about verbal communication, it's about all forms of communication. Fellas, when you are making love to your lady, listen to her. If you want to be one hell of a fantastic lover to her, you had better listen to her spiritually, verbally, and physically. The better you are at listening to her, the better you will be at making love to her—it's simple. Put another way, if you are able to listen effectively to her in living room, you will most certainly listen better in the bedroom. It's a tall order, fellas, but we can do it, trust me.

Through Our Eyes

If you could see you through our eyes
You would see how much you are a
Lovely prize.

If you could see you through our eyes
You would feel our hearts in your hands
This is love, a very special love, that comes
From a black man.

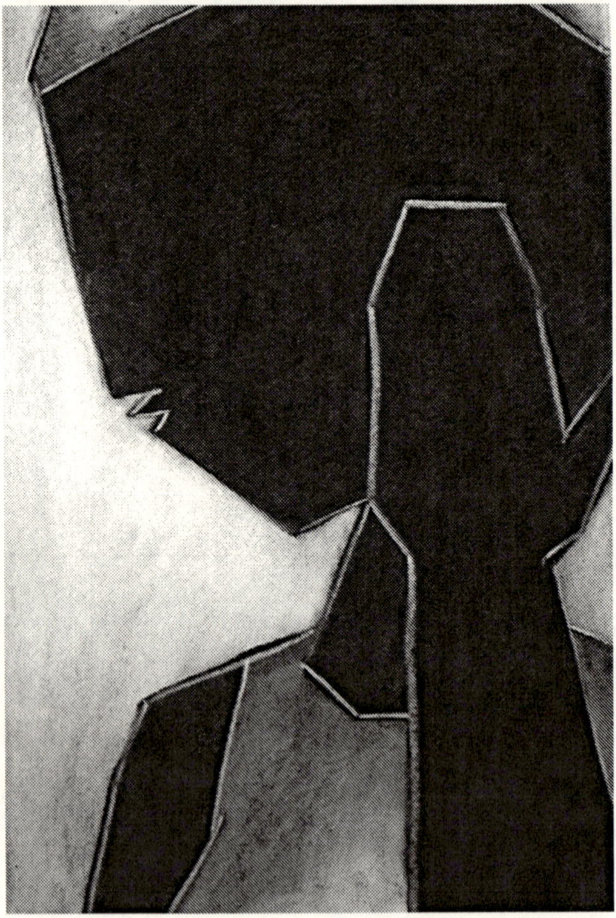

Chapter 9
Just Hold On

Keeping Your Faith and Hope

Ladies, I want to say a few words about Faith and Hope. Now I know that many of you have been hurt in ways that I can't even begin to imagine by shameless men who couldn't care less about your feelings or needs. Despite that, I am here to urge all of you to hold on to your faith and hope because faith is a good thing and let the truth be told—it's the only thing. I know that sometimes it feels next to impossible to believe that there are still good men out there that will love, respect, honor, and care for you; but ladies, they are out there and they are looking for you because we are on our way—believe it!

Finally, once again, I want to say to you what a good man will do. He will want to love you unconditionally and faithfully. A good man will care about how his words affect you. His touch will be soft and gentle. He will love you, sick or well, because he is a good man. A good man will put God into everything he says and does for you. Ladies, there may be times when you will catch him staring at you and you will ask him why is he staring. And he will say something like "Baby, you are such a pretty woman and I can't help but stare and count my blessings." Yes, he will sound something that.

The other day I was talking with a few of my guy friends and I asked them what would they want you ladies to know. The overwhelming consensus was that they wanted you to know just how much of a gift it is to have your love and respect. Ladies, do you know how good it is to know that you have our backs and that you will care for us whether we are sick or well? Do you know how much we care and love you all? What a gift indeed!

Ladies, when you are feeling down or alone, when you feel that there are no longer any good men out there, just know and believe that a good man is desperately looking for you and he is most certainly on his way. Just hold on a little bit longer; I promise we will get there.

If I Could Live My Life Again

If I could live my life again,
I would take more time to hold your
Hand.

If I could live my life again,
I would work even harder to
Be your man.

If I could live my life again,
I would whisper in your ear, my dear
And ask you to take my hand
And guide you to our private
Loveland.

If only I could live my Life
Again.

Chapter 10
Conclusion

To all of my wonderful Black Woman-Sisters, I just want you all to know that we are out here and we love you. Yes, many of us brothers have a ways to go, but I believe, as you also must believe, that we will someday get there.

Life is funny when you look at it. Everybody wants love, but as men, many of us are afraid of love. I truly believe that if you get anything out of life you have to be willing to put in the work, something too many men have been unwilling to do. In other words, we have to work together and love one another. This body of work is just my way of saying to all you wonderful Black Woman-Sisters out there that we love you and care about you and we need you.

I know that you may sometimes feel tired—then let us carry you for a while like you have carried us, and let us be good to you for a change. We really can, you know.

When you see or meet men that are trifling or dishonest, just remember and say to yourself, "I can and will do better." And above all, remember that he is nothing but a little boy in a man's body, because a real man won't treat you like that.

Finally, remember to always be good to yourself—even if you do it with a half-gallon of Ben and Jerry's, a battery-powered toy and a Chippendale's video—be good to yourself first, PLEASE!

A Message to All Women

Ladies, I feel that it is important to say a few words to all women everywhere. Now thus far, I have addressed the true greatness of my beautiful Black Woman-Sisters, but I would be a little remiss if I didn't say to you that when it comes to self-esteem, how you feel about yourself is extremely important no mater what race you are. This writer feels that all women should be treated with respect, love, and care. A man should never say anything to a woman that he would be ashamed to say if his mother were listening.

As I have said many times before, "The love of a good Black Woman-Sister is truly a gift to have and behold." There have been many, many times when I've seen one of my beautiful Black Woman-Sisters and I simply say to myself "There goes an intelligent and pretty black pearl," and in that moment, ladies, I feel that I am one of the luckiest men alive to behold such splendor.

Finally, I want you to know that I am so very grateful to all of the Black Woman-Sisters who have cared for me, loved, and blessed me. Simply, ladies, I am the man I am because of you.

Love, Kevin Waine

Research Methodology

A survey was furnished to 2,200 African-American men with a qualified age range of 18 to 65 years. The survey was conducted during the months of September, October, and November of 2001, and January and February of 2002. The survey respondents were contacted at the Los Angeles International, Oakland, Denver, and San Diego airports, in addition to various churches, colleges, and community organizations. The survey contained a total of 32 questions pertaining to the opinions of black men relating to the black woman.

The questions tested were a Z-test of proportions. The Z-test was selected due to the fact that the sample size was over 30. The level of significance used was 0.95 with a sample error of 0.10. Critical value of Z was calculated to be +/- 1.645, as this was a two-tailed test. The researcher received 2,013 completed surveys, which provided a 97% rate of return.

Finally, it should be noted that the survey data is limited based on the fact that only African-American men who could financially afford to fly were surveyed, thus this data may not be completely representative of the U. S. black male population at large.

Brown Sugar Pie Recipe

1 cup firmly packed brown sugar
1 tsp. Karo Syrup
1 egg, slightly beaten
1 tsp. vanilla
2 heaping tbsp. flour
3 tbsp. milk
2 tbsp. melted butter
4 oz. chocolate chips
1 prepared pastry pie shell

Very Special Ingredients:
Tender hugs
Thorough & tender foot massages
Hot candlelit dinner
Very warm almond oil (Rub gently)

Most important ingredient:
1 Strong black woman in any of the twenty-eight shades of black

Preheat oven to 350 degrees Fahrenheit. In a large bowl, combine the first six ingredients. Mix on medium speed for two minutes. Add chocolate chips and stir. Pour the mixture into the pie shell and bake for 35 minutes or until lightly browned and set. Remove from oven and let cool. Serve with whipped cream or ice cream. Note: This pie should been eaten slowly, patiently, and carefully in order to enjoy it fully.

A Very Special Thank You

Thank You, Melessa, for showing what a truly good woman is and how to be a good man.
You always believed in me.
With all my love,
K.W.

Be sure to look for Kevin's upcoming inspirational books:

Uncommon Valor

Kevin applauds the deep well of strength possessed by women struggling with breast cancer. He also speaks to men about how to be supportive of that special woman during such an ordeal.

The Greatness of Black Women II

In the second edition of this wonderful book, Kevin continues to show the world how special and fantastic the Black Woman-Sister is. In addition, look for his new inspirational series for women, *A Warm Bubble Bath for Her Heart*

Printed in the United States
95724LV00001B/116/A